PRAISE FOR *BEGINNING AND ENDING A PASTORATE*

With caring words and practical recommendations, experienced pastor and professor Bill Tuck offers keen insights for congregations and church leaders seeking to navigate the defining entries and exits of a pastor's journey with a community of faith. A worthy guide.

Daniel G. Bagby, PhD.
Emeritus Professor of Pastoral Care
Baptist Theological Seminary at Richmond

Just like sermons, pastorates need good beginnings and good endings. Building upon his own experiences in the pastorate, William Powell Tuck offers keen insight into the factors involved in making these good transitions happen. This book opens windows about what really goes on and what needs to go on during these transitions. This book shows sensitivity to all parties involved in these transitions and offers wise counsel to those serving interim pastorates. A superb read for all: young ministers ready to assume their first ministry assignments; those making mid-career changes; and those seeking to conclude their ministries in a wholesome way.

Michael G. Cogdill, DMin.
Campbell Divinity School
Buies Creek, N.C.

Tuck once again shares decades of insight and wisdom in the engaging and accessible *Beginning and Ending a Pastorate*. While this book provides sage counsel for times of pastoral transition, it actually is of great value for *all* pastors *and* congregations to read, study, and discuss - regardless of whether a pastorate is at its beginning, middle, or end. Eminently practical and deeply theological, Tuck's writing paints the picture of what it means to be a faithful pastor, and a faithful congregation.

Rev. Dr. Lolly Dominski, PhD.
Co-Pastor, Morton Grove Community Church
Adjunct Professor of Reformed Worship,
McCormick Theological Seminary

"Everything changes, nothing remains." says Heraclitus, my favorite philosopher. If this saying was true in Heraclitus' time, how much more true it is for us in our time! We live in a culture of constant change, and this is no less true for our congregations. The average pastorate last 5-7 years, meaning that for a pastor's 40-year career, they will say "Hello" and "Good-by" six to eight times each. A predecessor's healthy "good-by" can make the successor's "Hello" much more effective. A good word, said in season, may even endure beyond the pastoral transition. In this volume, Bill Tuck draws upon his wealth of experience as pastor, professor, consultant and interim, learning to say "Hello's" and "Good-by's" that are healthy and effective. Written in Bill's conversational style, it is a pleasure to read and a joy to learn.

Rev. Dr. David Moffett-Moore, PhD, D Min.
Pastor, Teacher, Author, Counselor,
United Church of Christ minister

Bill Tuck has given us another very practical and helpful tool for ministry. We are increasingly aware of the value of a healthy beginning and ending for pastoral ministry. Much of our work is focused upon these areas, and we are grateful for this new resource for ministers and churches entering those uncharted waters. Anyone about to enter or exit a congregation would be advised to read and learn from the wise voice of experience.

Bill Wilson, DMin.
Director, The Center for Healthy Churches

A Pastor Preaching: Toward a Theology of the Proclaimed Word

The Pulpit Ministry of the Pastors of River Road Church, Baptist (editor)

The Last Words from the Cross

Lord, I Keep Getting a Busy Signal: Reaching for a Better Spiritual Connection

Overcoming Sermon Block: The Preacher's Workshop

A Revolutionary Gospel: Salvation in the Theology of Walter Rauschenbusch

Holidays, Holy Days, and Special Days

A Positive Word for Christian Lamenting: Funeral Homilies

The Forgotten Beatitude: Worshipping through Stewardship

Star Thrower: A Pastor's Handbook

A Pastoral Prophet: Sermons and Prayers of Wayne E. Oates (editor)

The Abiding Presence: Communion Meditations

Which Voice Will You Follow?

The Difficult Sayings of Jesus

BEGINNING AND ENDING A PASTORATE

Conversations in Ministry Series, Volume 4

WILLIAM POWELL TUCK

Energion Publications
Gonzalez, FL
2018

ISBN10: 1-63199-556-1
ISBN13: 978-1-63199-556-9
Library of Congress Control Number: 2018909381

Energion Publications
P. O. Box 841
Gonzalez, FL 32560

energionpubs.com
pubs@energion.com
850-525-3916

To Ron Higdon
Fellow pastor and friend,
Who knows well
the beginning and ending of pastorates

TABLE OF CONTENTS

v

SERIES PREFACE

Parish ministry can be an exciting and challenging vocation. This has always been the case, but it is perhaps even truer today. At least in the European and North American contexts, institutional forms of religion are finding themselves pushed to the sidelines. Their purpose and value has been questioned, and with these questions come further questions about the professional status of those who are called to serve these congregations. A generation ago, congregational ministers might see themselves as members of a professional class, like that of medical doctors and attorneys. The Academy of Parish Clergy, the sponsor of this book series, was founded with just that vision—to encourage and enhance the professional practice of parish ministry. This was to be accomplished by setting professional standards, including the encouragement to engage in regular continuing education, and then providing a means of accountability to those standards. Although the broader culture has raised questions about the professional standing of parish clergy, the need for professional standards, continuing education, and accountability remains as important today as ever before. This is because the world in which ministry is being done is ever changing, and therefore clergy must adapt, learn new skills, and reposition themselves for a new day. It is helpful, therefore, to walk in the company of others who are also engaged in similar kinds of ministry.

What makes parish ministry both exciting and challenging is that most clergy are generalists. They're like the family practitioner, dealing with a wide variety of issues and people. No day is exactly the same, for they serve as teachers, preachers, worship leaders, providers of pastoral care, administrators, and social justice leaders. They may be more gifted in some areas than others, but ultimately, they find themselves engaged in a wide variety of tasks that often push them to the limits of ability and endurance. It is not a vocation that can be undertaken on one's own, and for a variety of reasons parish ministers need to find a community of others who share this calling, so that they might find encouragement, support, and ideas for dealing with parish life and ministry in the broader world.

Part of the founding vision of the Academy of Parish Clergy was to facilitate this need to find a community of peers, and with this in mind, Academy members were encouraged to create and join in Colleague Groups, where they could encourage one another and explore issues that confront clergy in their daily ministry, often using the "Case Study Method," which was emerging at the time among the professions. That model is still available, but it is the hope of the editors of this series that these books will also provide a foundation for conversation in clergy groups.

This vision continues to sustain the Academy more than forty years after its founding, and the APC book series, *Conversations in Ministry*, seeks to extend this vision by offering to clergy, books written primarily by practicing clergy for practicing clergy dealing with the issues that confront them in ministry today. Each book, published in partnership with Energion Publications, will be brief and focused (under 100 pages). Each book is designed to encourage reflection and conversation among clergy. The editors and authors of these books hope that the books will be taken up by groups of clergy and inspire conversation.

It is important to point out the use of the preposition "in." The conversations that are envisioned here are not simply about ministry, but are designed to emerge from within the context of ministry. Although the initial book covers a variety of issues facing clergy, future books will focus on specific issues including clergy ethics, self-care, preaching, worship leadership, congregational administration, use of social media. Each book will include discussion questions that can aid group conversation, but also individual reflection. Each book will reflect the purpose of the series, but each author will take the conversation in the direction the topic suggests.

May this series of books be a blessing to all who read them.

Robert D. Cornwall, APC
General Editor

ORIENTATION

The calling of a new pastor to a church is always a time of new beginnings and endings for a congregation. Sometimes, following a good experience with the present pastor who is leaving, the congregation likely has a positive feeling about the future. However, if the situation with the present pastor who is retiring or following a call to another church, or being forced to leave, has not been positive, the atmosphere of the congregation might be one of uncertainty, fear, hostility, confusion, or even despair. In my experience of fifty years as a pastor and interim and intentional interim pastor, I have found that preaching about the closing and beginning of a new chapter in the life of the congregation, during the last few weeks of my ministry there, can be helpful. Of course, consultation and discussion with the deacons, administrative committees, the Pastor Search Committee, and the congregation at large is vital. I have found that the closing sermons in my interim ministry, or my own pastorates, have been a positive way to focus on the important facts that I have addressed with committees, and the church as they anticipated the coming of a new pastor.

Some take a dim view of preaching and place little value on sermons. I have, however, experienced a different perspective on preaching and am still very positive about the effectiveness of well-prepared and biblically-focused sermons. The sermons in this book offer guidelines that a minister can present to a congregation in his or her last weeks with the church. The sermons seek to offer expectations and suggestions for the congregation about their pastor's role, and a perspective on ministry and the ministry of the congregation at large, as they seek to minister together. I have also found it helpful to engage in dialogue with the congregation about what I preached in these sermons. This kind of discussion enabled me to expound further, clarify, and answer questions that church members might have. After I preached the sermon, I furnished written copies of them for the congregation before the discussions.

This book is written with a particular focus for the Academy of Parish Clergy with whom I have been affiliated for many years now. I believe this work offers guidance for ministers who are beginning their ministries as well as those who are seeking to relocate in their ministry, and congregations that are confronting the leaving or calling of a new pastor. This book can be utilized by pastoral or ministerial study groups, and committees and congregations meeting in small groups as a study guide when they undertake the search for a new pastor. To me, pastoral ministry has been a deeply fulfilling calling that I would undertake again without any hesitation. I offer these sermons as one pastor's hope that they will assist pastors and congregations in making their ministry more effective and challenging as they serve our Lord together. Again, I express my sincere appreciation to my friend and fellow minister, Rand Forder, for proof-reading my manuscript.

CHAPTER 1

THE CALL TO MINISTER:
A PASTOR'S VIEW

EPHESIANS 3:7-12, 4:11-16

Several years ago, I heard Dr. Duke McCall, the former President of The Southern Baptist Theological Seminary, Louisville, Kentucky, tell of an experience that he had as a young student pastor in a country church. When he would finish speaking, one of his church members would come up to him and say one of two things to him: "Pastor, that was a good sermon" or "Pastor, that was a real good, uh, talk." This went on for several months, until Dr. McCall said he could stand it no longer. He went to the church member's farm and found him plowing in the field and asked him what he meant by his different responses.

"I can't stand it," Dr. McCall said. "I have to know the difference between sermon and talk."

The farmer replied: "Now pastor, I like you a lot, and I don't want to hurt your feelings. I'd rather not say."

"Well you are going to kill me with curiosity," Dr. McCall said, "if you don't tell me why you always hesitate and say one thing or the other."

"Okay, pastor," the farmer responded. "The difference as I see it is this: A sermon sounds better, but a talk says more."

A SENSE OF EXCITEMENT

I want to offer to you some suggestions as you prepare for the coming of your new pastor. I am not sure whether this is a sermon or a talk or maybe something in between. This Sunday and next Sunday I will attempt to share with you some things that I hope will be helpful to you as you prepare to minister together with your new pastor.

The church has had two years since our pastor retired and I have spent twenty months now in this interim time. Do you think that time has been wasted? Since Dr. Smith served as pastor here for eleven years, I believe it was appropriate to have a lengthy interim between him and the next pastor. Studies have indicated that if this does not happen, the pastor who comes too soon is often an interim himself or herself. Hopefully, this will not be the case here.

Your new pastor and his wife have not moved in over eleven years. I think they will discover that moving is not always easy. They will have spent a lot of time packing for the move. And I believe they will discover later that unpacking boxes will be a bit like Christmas morning. When they open a box, there are sometimes going to be surprised with what is in it. Hopefully, they will recognize their belongings, and at other times, they may simply wonder what has happened to them. They will be a long time getting settled in, so please be patient and help them as they work through their mound of boxes. Remember that moving is considered by many one of the worse stress factors that people can have. A friend of mine once said, "Hell is not a place, but a moving van." So, remember that moving is traumatic. Be patient with Dr. & Mrs. Jones. They will eventually get settled. It is a time of excitement for them and you, but also a time of adjustment.

GETTING TO KNOW ONE ANOTHER

There is no way that I can possibly address all of the matters that I would like to say to you in one sermon. I know that you are thankful I shall not attempt to do that. But over the next two Sundays I want us to examine a variety of ways that the New Testament speaks about the church and the ministry that we share in as followers of Christ.

I believe it is also very important for you and your new pastor to get some time to know one another. To be honest, he will not know many of you, though he will know some of you from these various meetings that we have had in church. It will not be easy for him to put his arms around 1300 people, but I believe that he will learn to do that one or two at a time. I believe that he will get to know you and love you, and that you will get to know him and love him and his family as well. He will not come as your pastor with all the answers to all of your spiritual problems, but he will come as a fellow pilgrim who is seeking to follow the leadership of Christ with you. He will come to minister with you as a part of the community of faith as you have need of his ministry.

Please tell him and his family your name several times. Don't assume that Charles and Donna will know your name after the first meeting. It will take some time. I remember a young man who came to the seminary several years ago when I was pastor at St. Matthews, Louisville, Kentucky. Every time he saw me as he came out of the door he said, "Dr. Tuck, my name is Jimmy Greer." Soon I knew who he was. Let me encourage you to do the same. Repeat your name again and again to your new pastor and his family.

THE FAMILY OF GOD

I know that he will come seeking to draw strength from you as his family of God. He will minister to you in times of special needs, but I also believe that you will likewise minister to him and his family. While I was pastor in Bristol, Virginia, my wife, Emily, experienced the death of both of her parents. That congregation ministered to us in our grief. They were church to us. We felt the embrace of that congregation as they lifted us up in time of need. When I was pastor in North Carolina, both of my parents died while I was there. That congregation likewise ministered to us during the time of grief. I believe with genuine confidence that in times of joy and sorrow, you will be family and church to your pastor and his family.

Allow him the needed time to be with his own family as well. He will need many nights, meal times, days off, and other special times to do his own family thing, maybe taking his children to school or picking them up, attending PTA meetings, taking family vacations, after school ball games, concerts, etc. Remember his wife, Donna, may have her own career and will need time to do her "thing." She will offer her gifts, but permit her to serve in her way and in her best time. Don't let your pastor work too hard. He needs some time off. Encourage him to take it. He will be a better pastor because of it. I often found myself working seven days a week without any time off. I never had a layperson say to me, "Pastor, you are working too hard. Take some time off!" But I probably needed someone to say that. Why don't you be that voice for your pastor if he needs to hear that helpful word?

THE PREACHER'S STORY

I believe that all authentic preaching in ministry is autobiographical. There is the gospel, but there is, as Paul said, "My gospel." Each of us shares his or her insight into the gospel. Dr. Jones will share with you out of his pilgrimage as a Christian, out of his understanding of the way the Good News breaks into our lives with hope and redemption. I know that he will seek to be open with you and vulnerable with you. He will be transparent. What you see, I believe, will be what he is. He will come to you as a fellow human being. He is not a superman. He will not be able to walk on water. He will make mistakes and not have all of the answers. Although he may have a high energy level and may be a "workaholic," I believe that he will also at times get tired, sleepy, and sometimes irritable and maybe even become discouraged. He is human like you and like me. He will need time off; he will need some time for rest, play, recreation, and some time alone and some time with his family.

THE PASTOR COMMITS HIS OR HER GIFTS

In our scripture passage for today, Paul speaks about the variety of gifts within ministry. Your new pastor will bring you his variety of gifts and so will his wife and children. He will come committing to you the gift of ministry which he has. I believe that the highest gift that anyone can give to another is his or her own individuality. Celebrate and affirm his unique gifts. No one preacher can ever fulfill every expectation. I hope that you will not expect him to be a "cookie-cutter copy" or "carbon copy" of some other preacher in the past or present, but will allow him to proclaim to you the truth of God as he understands it through his own personality. I am convinced that on the day of judgment, as your pastor stands before God, he is not going to ask him, "Charles Jones, why were you not like Moses or Elijah or Paul or Dr. Lewis or Dr. Smith or Dr. Tuck?" Instead I believe God will ask: "Did you use to the best of your ability the gifts which I gave you in ministry for me?" I hope that he will be able to say, "Yes, Lord, I gave you the best gifts I had to offer."

A VARIETY OF GIFTS

Paul spoke about a variety of gifts: some apostles, some prophets, some evangelists, some pastors, and teachers. He had just been writing about the unity of the Church but that did not mean uniformity. Our unity is in a common sharing in ministry, but each one makes his or her unique contribution to the total ministry of the Church. In the early church these individuals fulfilled special functions in the use of their gifts. They represented a number of different persons serving in special ways. But I do not think I distort the meaning of this passage, which depicts various functions in specialized ministries, when I draw upon it for reflections of what effective pastoral ministry should be. These are essential ministries that are still needed in the life of the Church today.

The apostles were an important group in the early Church and had a special place because they had seen Jesus Christ. This group included more, however, than the twelve disciples. Barnabas, James, the brother of Jesus, Silvanus, Andronicus, Junia, and Paul were persons who had seen Christ personally and had been a witness to His resurrection. Soon, however, this group would die. But is there not a sense in which this requirement is still essential for the Church to continue? Only those who have known Christ can share Him with others. There is a real sense in which all followers of Jesus are "apostles," ones sent, to bear witness to an experience with a living Lord.

At the heart of our faith is the belief that it is essential to have a personal experience with Christ before Church membership. Before we can share Christ with others, we must have met Him ourselves. A social worker asked a young boy one day why his parents had not taught him to read. "Sir," he responded, "you can't give what you ain't got, any more than you can go back to where you've never been!" We cannot be sent, if we have not met the one who sends.

A PROPHETIC WORD

There is also a dimension of the prophet in ministry. No one can really like being a prophetic voice. His words are often disturbing. A prophet is not so much one who is foretelling as one who is forth telling. His primary concern is not with the future but with the impact of the "Word from God" on the present. The prophet comes to exhort, edify, and sometimes comfort us with how the Word from God touches our lives.

The Word of God addresses not just our private or personal life, but it is concerned with all of our lives—our social life as well as our personal life. God's prophetic word sits in judgment on our political and economic way of life. The word judges us in our moral behavior but also our attitude and action in war, pollution, discrimination, poverty, child abuse, and many other areas. God lifts His standard up before us and says that we have not measured up; we have fallen short; we have missed the mark. We have evaded the goal for the higher good and have often twisted the means to reach less than worthy aims.

A FREE PULPIT

Your new pastor will come to a church where the pulpit has been a "free" pulpit. As he understands the Word of God, he will declare it to you. He will not claim to have all of the truth or the only understanding into truth, but he will share with you his understanding of God's truth as he has perceived it. I hope that you will give him the freedom to do that and the freedom to proclaim that truth as God has gifted him through his own preaching style.

I heard about a minister who said that he had been pastor of a church for 25 years. He said in all of those years, he told a friend, "I have never had one word of criticism." "Nobody ever criticizes an echo," his friend responded.

I know that Dr. Jones will not seek simply to be an echo, reflecting from you what he hears you say. I believe that he will strive to discern what God's Word of direction and guidance is for this congregation to live as God's children. Sometimes that means that he will comfort the afflicted and at other times, afflict the comfortable.

A RESPONSIBLE PULPIT

In all of your pastor's prophetic preaching, I know that he will also speak as one who acknowledges that God's judgment first addresses him and his sense of his own weaknesses. Any prophetic word will also be spoken in anguish not in anger. He will weep with you for your sins. I believe he will constantly be reminding you of your joint responsibility unto God. He will weep because the Word judges a nation and people that he loves. I know that it will not be easy to hear that word. I know that he will try to share the prophetic Word not with denunciation but with directions, not with irresponsible criticism, but with an informed corrective, not with harsh, superior judgment but with a supportive concern. With the freedom of this pulpit, I believe that he will also recognize the twin need of responsibility.

EVANGELISM

We are also called to be evangelists. I make no apologies for that role. An essential part of the ministry of the Church is to share and spread the Good News of Christ. In the early days of the New Testament Church, the evangelists were probably more like our missionaries today who carried the Word for the first time to those in some other land who had never heard of Jesus Christ. As Paul told young Timothy, "Do the work of an evangelist" (2 Timothy 4:5). One of the primary purposes of your pastor's ministry and the ministry of this congregation is to present the Good News about Christ so men and women will put their trust in God through Him and accept Him, as Savior and follow Him as Lord through His Church.

Several years ago, a woman was on a tour group in Westminster Abbey. As they were guided through that magnificent cathedral, she observed the tombs of famous kings, poets, great scholars, and others. She seemed totally unimpressed. Finally, she turned to the tour leader and said, "I've got a question I want to ask." "What is it?" he responded. "Has anybody been saved here lately?" she asked.

It is a question the Church needs constantly to keep before itself. We are commissioned to spread the Good News of God's saving grace. We have a magnificent, air-conditioned, comfortable building. The question we need to keep before us is: Will this building be simply a place of beauty and majesty or will it be a place where men and women and young people can feel that they have been addressed by God? Will it be a place where those without direction will find for the first-time guidance, wholeness, and redemption? Will those who have fallen feel the Christ who lifts them up? I hope our church will be a place where Christ comes to bring a new beginning for a defeated life; encouragement for the lonely; insight for the confused; direction for the searcher; hope for the discouraged; and salvation for the lost. I hope that you and your pastor will share with boldness the Good News of the salvation that we experience through Jesus Christ.

PASTOR AND TEACHER

The roles of teacher and pastor also loom large in Paul's words. In the Greek text, teacher and pastor are linked together, and it is difficult to separate these two functions totally. Both are essential in the life of an effective church. As your chief teacher and preacher among many other teachers, I hope that you will give Dr. Jones time to study and prepare what he would share with you. No one can have a word worthy of sharing if he does not give himself or herself time to study. I hope that you will give Him a set number of hours each day, which he will determine for study, that he might probe and reflect on the word of God. This will give him an opportunity to study the theological works that he will need to sense and understand more clearly what God has to say to us today.

F.W. Robertson, the famous 19th century preacher, once observed: "I can never light my own fire." Most of us have our theological fires lit by someone else as they ignite us through our study, reflection, and prayer. In this study time, your new pastor needs the opportunity to probe deeply into his own spiritual life, to deepen and develop it so that he might seek to lead you in your own spiritual enrichment. Please give him that necessary time.

If you ever call and the secretary or someone else says, "I am sorry the pastor is studying right now. Could you call back later?" I hope you will not consider that a waste of time. Study time is essential if your pastor is going to be an effective preacher and teacher. If we had only 100 people gathered in this congregation each week, in a year's time that would aggregate to 5,000 man/ woman hours per year. That is a lot of time. Your pastor will not want to waste your time when you come together, so he will prepare carefully what he wants to share with you each week. His preparation will take time, effort, and energy in his study to be a useful and constructive minister of the Word.

THE PASTORAL ROLE

The preaching and pastoral roles are joined together. I know that I, myself, have learned much about how to preach as I have walked with church members in their grief and during other times in their lives. I have held the hands of those who were dying and those who were grieving. I have embraced people in times of loneliness and desperation. As a pastor, I participated with people in times of joy and agony, hope and despair, frustration and dreaming. I know that your new pastor will want to reach out to you during those times and be your pastor. I hope that you will give him the opportunity to do your funerals and weddings so that he will learn to know you and love you and you in turn will grow to love him. It is during these times he can build a special relationship with you and your family.

In a congregation of this size it is impossible for your new pastor to minister to everyone at once. But there are several other staff members here and they will all share in ministry together. Laypersons, also, will respond. Even when your pastor cannot be there personally with you, he will always be informed about your need or your joy by a staff member and shall be involved with you by empathy, concern, and prayer. He is not a mind reader, so don't expect him or some other staff member to try and guess when you have a special need. Keep him and others informed. Let the church know when there is an opportunity for service so that he can minister to your needs.

EQUIPPING THE CHURCH FOR SERVICE

Notice that Paul insists that the ministries of the apostles, prophets, evangelists, pastors, and teachers are all to equip the church for service. One of your pastor's chief functions, as I sense it from Paul's description here, is to be an equipper—one who seeks to train others in the ministry of Christ in the world. There is no way that one person can do, nor should do, the entire ministry in this congregation. There is no way that the staff can do all of the ministries. Every person in this congregation is a minister. Each person needs to fulfill his or her place in service through this church. There are so many gifts and abilities in this congregation, and we need to draw upon the wide resources.

No one expects the Dean of a medical school to perform all the operations and other practices of medicine in a community. She trains others to do that. No one expects the President of a seminary to do all the preaching and pastoral work in a community. He engages with other professors to train other ministers to have a more expanded and effective ministry. One of the major responsibilities of your new pastor is to help train and equip others for ministry. That will be one of his most important goals here at First Baptist Church.

THE PASTOR'S CALLING TO SERVE

There is no question in my mind that your pastor believes that his essential calling is to serve as a follower of Christ. When graduates received their degrees from the Baptist Theological Seminary at Richmond, one of the things they received in addition to their diploma was a towel. The school gave students that towel as a reminder that they were called, not to be a boss or a ruler, but to be a servant. Your pastor is aware that our Lord has said that "the greatest of all is the servant of all." He has come to this church to minister, to be a servant of Christ, not a servant of people but a servant of Christ to minister in His name.

I know that he will pour himself into this ministry. I hope that you will seek to protect him, also, so that he will not "burn himself out." One of the difficult things in ministry is a person can pour himself into his job so much that he can reach the point that he has no more to give. You can assist him by encouraging him to take a day off, to take vacation time, to spend time with his family, to have other recreational pursuits in his life. He will minister more effectively to you if you allow him time to develop his own life in a way that is full, round, and complete. He is a servant of God, but he is a human being with all kinds of needs. Be a friend to your pastor, his wife, and children. Ministry can be lonely. They need and desire your friendship. Invite him and his family into your home for a meal or out for a meal.

THE PASTOR'S BLOG OR PARAGRAPH IN THE CHURCH NEWSLETTER

I personally believe that a pastor's online blog and his or her pastoral paragraph in the church newsletter are special ways to communicate with the congregation. Many persons today use the internet to keep up with the news, and the use of a blog or a paragraph on the church's webpage can offer an opportunity for the pastor to state his or her views, ideas, hopes, dreams, interpretations of Scripture or theological or denominational issues, personal concerns or a hundred other matters about the church or other things. Many today will go online for information before they will read anything in print. Before personal blogs became popular, I utilized a weekly pastor's paragraph in our church newsletters called "The Friar's Fragment." This was an excellent vehicle for me to keep my church informed about what was happening in our congregation, my position on church related or theological issues, biblical interpretations, current ethical or social issues that I addressed, and numerous other matters. I discovered that many in my congregations not only read them faithfully, but shared many of them with their family and friends. Encourage your pastor to use one or both of these important instruments of communication, and grant him or her the freedom to share their perspective with you.

LET'S EQUIP OURSELVES

Let us not forget why we are equipping ourselves. I heard about a young man that could not pass a college without enrolling in another course. There comes a point when one needs to stop enrolling in courses and start producing a living. There are some people in churches who are always going to meetings and getting more training but never use it for anything. We are being trained and equipped to serve— to be in the world as the Body and people of Jesus Christ.

When Eric Sevareid reached the time of retiring as a news commentator, he reflected about his years in Washington, D.C. and a fellow commentator who also worked there. He said that this man knew all the important people: the President, the senators, the President's cabinet, the diplomats, the bureaucrats, and the socially elite. He had the right contacts and the essential information. But he had one problem. He never used what he had. "He forgot what he was here for." What good does all the training and enabling do if they are not used in the world serving in the name of Jesus Christ? We are equipped to be Christ's loving, caring, ministering people in the world today. We are called to be servants. We follow our Lord who came to minister and *not* be ministered to.

MATURING IN THE FAITH

Paul notes that the Body of the Church is to be growing toward maturity in the faith. We are to move beyond childish understanding of the faith to "the stature of the fullness of Christ" or "mature manhood." These expressions are images of maturity. We are not to be like those who are unstable and are tossed and driven like a ship in the waves or have such childish gullibility that we are carried away by every new wind of false teaching. In this church, we shall share the Good News of Christ to those who may never have heard it before. But we also want this to be a congregation where, once men and women have heard the Good News, they can continue to grow and mature in the faith. The church is not *just* a birthing ward but a place where Christians are nurtured and developed.

A Christian is always on a pilgrimage to be more like the Master. Once we have experienced new birth we are in a life of growth. We are always in the process of becoming more like Christ. We know that we never arrive but are continually striving to be like our Lord. In our journey of faith, we can face the toughest of questions, whether they rise from science, philosophy, or the struggles of life, because we have a faith that is founded on truth, and we are open to all questions that will enable us to understand the truth better. In seeking a mature faith, we can confront all the testing that will come to our faith, because we worship a God who is founded on the truth and is sufficient to meet our every need. I know your new pastor will do this. Join with him in this important journey.

THE CHURCH IS MEASURED BY CHRIST.

As we grow toward a mature faith, Paul reminds us that Christ is the head of the Church, and all things are measured by him. When we are properly joined to Christ, that point of contact determines who and what we are and leads us on to be much more than we already are. The development and growth of the Church is under the direction of Christ. We labor in the Church not for our glory but His. I used to remind my students at the seminary that our goal in preaching is not that people will say, "Isn't he or she a great preacher!" but "Isn't it a great *gospel!*" We seek through our service to point people to Christ who is Head of the Church. I know your new pastor will seek to do that. Labor with him toward that high goal.

THE CHURCH—HOTEL OR HOSPITAL

Several years ago, I heard Dr. Findley Edge, former Professor of Religious Education at The Southern Baptist Theological Seminary,

Louisville, Kentucky, preach and ask the question: "Is our church primarily a hotel or a hospital?"

A hotel exists primarily for the paying guest. Everything is done in building a hotel, the decorations, the furniture, as well as the servers of the hotel, to make the paying guests comfortable and happy. Everything is done that would make the hotel appealing; the décor is that which would be attractive; the furniture is comfortable. Everything is done for the benefit of the paying guests. If anything happens when we are the paying guests in a hotel that we don't like, for example if the air conditioning is not working, we immediately call down to the desk and say, 'I want to speak to the manager.' Then if the matter is not fixed, we have a very good way of letting our displeasure be known. We don't go back. We withhold our business.

If the church is a hotel, then the church exists primarily for the paying guest—that is you. You are the ones who are paying for this magnificent building. If the church is viewed primarily as a hotel, then everything that is done here is done for your benefit. The beauty of it is the kind of thing that will be attractive and appealing to you. The types of sermons that are preached are the type you enjoy. The kind of music that is sung is the kind you enjoy. The other activities that are held here are the kind of activities that you enjoy.

If the church is like a hotel, the pastor will be comparable to the hotel manager. He is responsible for all of the operations. If something happens in the church that you don't approve, then you let the pastor know. I let him know if I don't like his sermons or if he preaches too long. I let him know that the building is too hot or too cold or let him know that I don't like the music, what the choir sings, or if don't care for the hymns the congregation sings. Whatever it is, we owe the pastor a response. If the matter is not corrected to our satisfaction, we have a good way of letting it be known that we don't like it. We quit coming. We withhold our giving.

But if the church is more like a hospital, it will exist primarily for sick people. Everything that is done in a hospital is done for the benefit of the sick people—the type of beds that are used, the way the rooms are arranged around the nurse's station and the like. All of this is for the benefit of sick people, so they can be served most effectively. If, indeed, the church is a hospital, the sick people all around us are evidently are not aware of it because they are not coming here to get well. They simply do not know that we are in the business of trying to help sick people get well. If the church is a hospital, the staff ministers are the resident physicians and the interns are all of God's people who are in training to become minister physicians. Now the question is, 'Are we, who are in the church, really learning how to become physicians, or is what we are doing just coming here to the hospital to have a weekly meeting between the resident physicians and the interns and talk about how sick the world is?'

Dr. Edge uses this analogy as sort of a parable about the church. We need to discern whether the church is primarily here simply to meet our needs or whether the church exists to reach out to those who need to hear the Good News of Jesus Christ. We are all "sick" in some way. We need healing. The church is more than just a place to make us comfortable and where we should feel good. The church has been called to minister in the world. If we really understand the life and ministry of Jesus, I believe that we need to be concerned about the needy, the hurting, the lonely, the outcast, the unloved—all of the people in the world. We need to minister to them and draw them so that they can find healing in the arms of Jesus Christ our Lord.

My prayer is that when your new pastor comes, this wonderful church will not be a hotel, but a hospital where people can find the healing love of God and the redemption that God's grace gives to us. May God grant that the coming of your new pastor will be a time of excitement and recommitment so that you will work with him to serve God more faithfully.

PASTORAL PRAYER

Eternal God, we gather today to acknowledge a new chapter in the life of this congregation will begin soon. We thank you for all the dedicated service which has gone before us by former pastors, staff and good lay people. This church has been blessed by them and we are grateful for their sacrifice of love.

As we look to the future, teach us how to serve you more faithfully, share the Good News of Christ more easily with others, and bear the burdens of one another more cheerfully and to love each other more fully.

As this congregation looks to the future with a new pastor, teach us how to get to know one another better and work together in Your name and seek to grow in the grace and knowledge of Christ. Bless Charles Jones and his family and the unique gifts they bring. May we love and support them as they begin their ministry with us. Help us to learn from one another, affirm the gifts we recognize in others and support each other with genuine love. Let this be a time of new beginnings, new visions, new hopes, and a time of forgiving old quarrels, hurts, gossip or words of criticism. Knit us together as your children, bonded together in love, as we lean on Christ, the Head of the Church.

Bless now those who are ill, grieving, lonely, or in distress. May Your strong grace be real to them. We bow before You now in expectation. We know You are here. Help us to sense Your presence. Amen.

ACTION AND REFLECTION

Ask your focus group to compile a list of what they believe are the main jobs of a pastor. Reflect on how your former pastor fulfilled this list, and note which areas seemed to be more essential than others. Comment on how you will respond if your new pastor has only some of these qualifications.

DISCUSSION:

1. What do you think is the most important gift your new pastor can bring to the church?

2. Which is more important, the preaching or pastoral ministry?

3. What do you think "freedom of the pulpit" means? In what ways can the pastor violate this role?

4. What is the pastor's responsibility in equipping the congregation for ministry?

5. How do you see the ministry of the church in today's world?

CHAPTER 2

THE CALL TO MINISTER:
PARTNERS IN SERVICE

PSALM 100; EPHESIANS 4:11-17

The British novelist, J. B. Priestly, was once invited to write a short article on his religious beliefs. He declined saying that, at the moment, he was perhaps better able to deny than to affirm beliefs. But he said almost wistfully, "I regret this because now is the time for gigantic affirmations."

It is so easy to stand outside and criticize the Church. It is natural, when you are a pastor and when you have taught in a seminary, to be critical of the Church. No one sees its weakness any more clearly than the pastor who serves within its walls. I do not minimize the problems and difficulties, but I have seen the strengths as well and take pride in those who serve Christ through His church. I don't focus on merely an ideal view of the Church. I know the not-so-holy-local church, warts and all. There is so much more to affirm about the church than there is to deny or to criticize. As you prepare for the coming of your new pastor, Dr. Charles Jones, let me share with you several ways you can minister effectively together in service for Christ through this church. Here are few of the affirmations which I feel we can attest to today.

THE LAITY

One of the things I have learned to affirm about the Church is the lay persons who work in the church. I know your new pastor, Charles Jones, will join me in this affirmation. I really like lay people. I even like deacons! There are some pastors who seem to have an adversarial relationship with their lay workers and particularly with deacons. I remember, even as a small boy, having a sense of awe about the folks who took up the offering, sang in the choir, and taught Sunday School classes. They seemed to be people who stood apart in some way from the rest of us.

I remember vividly the impact many lay persons had upon my life. I will never forget Mr. Martin, who taught my junior Sunday School class, and talked to us about what Jesus Christ meant to him. He could not even read. Someone else would read the Sunday School lesson and then, he would tell us what it meant. I can still see Louise, Eunice, and Tillie Drapper as they worked with us as young people in Training Union. I remember Mrs. Templeton who led the Youth Choir and made us excited about music and the Christian faith. I can still see Mrs. Lucille Harvey who worked year after year in Vacation Bible School. I can't forget Billy Wood, who used to be the director of Training Union. He helped me when I was youth pastor in my home church.

I remember when I went off to college, the excitement that was created for me by the homes that were opened to me by lay persons who invited me to share a meal and see something of their home life. This was a welcomed respite in what was for me a strange and alien community. Dr. James Zambus was a college dean who encouraged a young preacher to keep on studying when the way was hard.

In my first church I remember walking out in the plowed field with Joe and Christine Good and hearing them talk about God, their church, and their farm life. They offered me words of hope and encouragement. Bob and Madeline Booker opened their home to a college boy preacher and let me spend the night with them.

They entertained the revival preacher and their pastor for a whole week in their home. Bud Lowe and countless others invited me to eat at their tables which were covered with dozens of vegetables and two or three different kinds of meat. I remember James Sparks who was a carpenter and a deacon, and the guidance he gave me in learning how to "build" a church. He, along with many others in that community, enriched my life.

I recall going to a college church and discovering a young man named John Honeycutt, who wanted to see how we could take the power of the gospel and relate it to the underprivileged and the needy. I can still see college students beginning to come into our church to find ways to minister to the poor and needy while they were in college. I can see a shipbuilder named Riley Lee, who directed our church choir because we couldn't afford a full-time director at that particular time. I saw Pam Pace, who week after week, added beauty to our church with what she did with flowers for the Sunday Service. Margaret Myers took over our church kitchen and fed hundreds of people and made table ministry a meaningful way of serving Christ.

Others come to mind. Lionel Pruner retired as manager of a dairy company and began a lay ministry in nursing homes. I can still see Bea Hulsey, who stood six feet four inches, reach down to help small boys learn about the Christ-like way. Years later, after serving as their teacher, he welcomed back grown men who thanked him for his ministry. I remember Mrs. Rose who taught preschool children for fifty years. I watched Jim and Polly St. Martin open their home to strangers and newcomers in the community. Jim never knew who Polly might invite home to their table. He might arrive home at night and there would be two or three strangers around his table. This was one of their ways of sharing their faith with others. I can still see Connie Glass and Hershel Minor "signing" to those who were deaf, so they could "hear" the gospel of Christ.

I remember hearing a "deacon of the week" tell of an experience he had when he received a phone call at two o'clock in the morning from one of our church members who said that she had a flat tire and wondered if he would come and help. He thought it was just a part of the "deacon of the week" responsibility. He didn't know that she thought she had called the AAA road service. But he went!

Down through the years I affirm the ministries I have seen lay persons and deacons perform in the church. They are often the people who really carry on much of the church's ministry. Many find their places and serve faithfully. I am proud to talk about what others like this have contributed to my life. When your new pastor gets to know you better he will discover, as I have, the various kinds of ministries in which you are engaged in this fine church.

THE CALLED-OUT ONES

We all need a sense of call to some kind of ministry. If I were to ask today, "How many of you are ministers?" I wonder how many hands would go up. Usually we think of only the "professional" folks as the ministers. The rest of us are lay persons. But, think with me a moment. What is a lay person? I am a layman in many respects. You sure don't want me performing brain surgery or operating on you for a kidney stone! I am a novice in those areas.

I remember hearing a lecture on symbolic logic, and although I was majoring in Philosophy of Religion in graduate school, this man, who was a mathematician, spoke so abstractly that I could not begin to follow him. In the area he was addressing, I was a layman and could not begin to understand it. In many areas I am not skilled. I cannot read electrical blueprints or build computers. I am a lay person in those areas.

EVERYONE HAS A MINISTRY

When it comes to being a part of the Church, the New Testament says that we are the laity—the people of God, the called-out ones, and all of us share in ministry. On this Pentecost Sunday, remember that God poured His Spirit upon all the Believers who were gathered in one place. Not a few but *all*. Ministry is not just for the professionals, but every single one of us has his or her ministry in the Church. Too often, many in the Church think that to be a lay person means that one can sit back and simply leave ministry to others. That's not to understand what the New Testament means by ministry.

I remember watching a basketball game once on television where two coaches got in such an argument in the middle of the court that they were pushing each other back and forth, up and down the floor, while they were arguing with each other. The players gathered around them and began to encourage them. Soon the spectators began to yell and encourage them on. The referees stood hopelessly by and could do nothing. But there was something wrong with that action in a basketball game. You do not *have* a basketball game when the two coaches are in the middle of the court arguing. The players need to be out there playing.

The work of ministry is not carried on just by the professional people but by *all* of us. Every person in this church has a place in ministry. Each and every one of us needs to find his or her place of ministry in the Church of Christ. You have a gift of ministry, and you need to discover what it is, if you have not done that already. Your new pastor cannot do all the church's ministry nor should he.

Dr. Gordon Kingsley, former President of William Jewell College, told me about the time his father began his ministry in a small little Missouri town. He was on fire with the gospel message and with a sense that all Believers were ministers. He started preaching that message and teaching that message to that church. The members were not quite ready for it.

Therefore, he was called aside by the senior deacon in the church, a wonderful man who was trying to "father" his dad's spirit by saying something like this: "Son, we hired you to do the preaching and we hired you to lead the singing and we hired you to do the praying, because not many of us pray out loud, and we hired you to do the visiting. Son, if you do those things, we will do the paying. And let me tell you, son — we have had preachers before you came, and we are going to have preachers like you after you have gone, so don't get too excited about anything and we'll all get along just fine." Gordon said, "I saw my dad cry twice in his short life. Twice. And this was one of the times."

Do you understand why? He had a sense that these were the people of God called to do the work of God, and he was suddenly being told that he was their theological hit-man, their hired gun to do the church work while they carried on their spectator religion. You are sensitive and sophisticated not to say that to Dr. Jones, and I advise you not to try it. But if you should ever have some hint or a whisper or an iota of a thought in that direction, drive it from your mind and heart, for it is sin. It is corrupt. God has committed to us—all of us—the ministry of reconciliation. Be willing to bear your load and your share.

THE VARIED MINISTRIES OF THE CHURCH

How many kinds of ministry can this church have? It is un-limited! You are already engaged in some: missions, music, youth, children's work, and teaching. Our ministries are limited only by your gifts as you contribute them to Christ through this church, and by our imagination. You are a minister as well as those of us on the professional staff, and each needs to assume his or her place of service. There is a great variety of ministries. I hope that you will find your ministry, and that you will become excited about your opportunity to work and grow.

There are really no hierarchies in ministries. There is not one that is more important in the eyes of God than others. None of us is supposed to be just consumers. None of us can be spectators and observers.

I like the way that Karl Barth wrote about this a number of years ago when he said: "There can be no talk of higher and lower order of specific service. There is differentiation of functions, but the preacher cannot really stand any higher than the other elders; nor the bell-ringer stand lower than the Professor of Theology.

There can be no 'clergy' and no 'laity' no merely 'teaching' and no merely 'listening,' Church, because there is no member of the Church who is not the whole thing in his own place."[1]

EVERY CHRISTIAN A PRIEST

Each of us is the church in a particular spot. Every Christian is a priest. You need to find your place of ministry. The Church of the Savior in Washington, D.C., affirms in their membership statement that the Church of Christ is a ship on which "there are no passengers, all are crew members." Every single Christian needs to be engaged in ministry. If we are a member of the Christ's Church, a member of this congregation, then we need to find what our ministry is and in what way we can serve and be a part of the vital Body of Christ.

One of my favorite theologians is Charles Schulz, which may indicate something about my theological level, but I do admire him. In one of Schulz's cartoons, Snoopy is beginning to jog and, as he is running, his body begins to talk to him. His feet say, "Man, don't you know what you are doing to me? You are killing me! I can't take this." Soon the calf muscles say, "Well, man, it's kind of tough on us, too." Then the thigh muscles begin to respond, "Well, it's really us that are keeping you going." Soon the arms say, "Well, I give you motion and activity. You have to have me." And the lungs say, "Without our ability to breath you can't make it." Finally, the heart speaks, "If I stop all of you have had it." As Snoopy finally climbs back upon his doghouse later he comments, "All are necessary. Every one of you guys is important."

Every single one of us has a ministry. You need to find through this church, and in it, your place to minister in the name of Jesus Christ. None of us can be just a passenger on the ship of Christ. We are called to be a vital part of the ministry of Christ.

---

1   Barth, Karl. Article for The Universal Church in God's Design, quoted in The Realm of Redemption by J. Robert Nelson (Greenwich: The Seabury Press, 1951), 145.

Some Ways to Help Your New Pastor

If you recall, I said last Sunday that I was going to try to share several sermons with you about ways you and your new pastor, Dr. Charles Jones, might minister effectively together. There is, of course, no way I can say all the things I want to say about the responsibility of church members. But let me suggest a few things you can all do to make the church's ministry and the pastor's ministry better.

Be Faithful in Your Attendance

1) *Learn to be faithful in your attendance.* There is nothing more discouraging to the church than poor attendance. Oh, I know you have to have some vacation. We all take some time away. We are not saying never take a weekend. Everyone needs some time apart. But remember that your spiritual growth will depend upon your sense of faithfulness in worship and in your other church ministries.

Be Faithful and Diligent in Your Ministry

2) When you find your place of ministry and you commit your life to it in this church, then *be faithful and diligent in it.* Do not take a place of service and then come only half the time and not be dependable. Take your end of the load and bear it up. Carry your responsibility with commitment and grace.

Be an Active Listener

3) *Be an active listener.* Preaching is not really a monologue. It should be a dialogue. Your pastor wants to hear you! He wants to hear your concerns, your aches, and your questions. Jot them down on a piece of paper and hand them to him or mail or email them to him. If you have an idea, quotation, or something that you want to share with him, get it to him. If there is a book that has excited you, or some questions you have about the faith or theology, feel

free to let him hear from you. He may not be able to answer all your questions, but I know he will take them seriously.

Remember that your part in listening means that you must work at it. As Reuel Howe says the laity has a responsibility for the delivery of the minister's sermon. One day a layman came out of church and said to his preacher: "We didn't do so well today."

"What do you mean?" the pastor asked.

"I mean," the layman said, "your sermon was not as helpful as it might have been because I wasn't working along with you. In fact, I think I was pushing down the meaning of something that happened to me this past week."[2]

Preaching is a cooperative venture between preacher and laity. You need to be active listeners because your role helps or hurts preaching. I could go into congregations when I was a supply preacher and tell what kind of preaching and listening went on in that congregation. All you had to do was sit there or come into the pulpit and you could tell very quickly whether the people and pastor were sharing together in dialogue. I hope you and your new pastor will.

ENCOURAGE EACH OTHER

4) I hope that we shall also engage in a ministry of concern. I pray that you and your new pastor will learn to *encourage each other*. Just as Barnabas was called the Son of Encouragement in the early Church, we need more encouragers in the Church today. We need more men, women, and young people who will say a good word to help another along the way. Oh, it is so easy to say something negative, to be a critic or to point out what is wrong with the new pastor or the Church, but to give your life in service, to get involved in the Church, and to help somebody else is a marvelously different story.

I will never forget the encouragement a lay person gave me every Sunday. Even if I thought I had really bombed on Sunday,

2   Howe, Reuel L. *Partners in Preaching: Clergy and Laity in Dialogue* (New York: The Seabury Press, 1967), 91.

this layman would come by the door and always find some good words to say to encourage me. It was a great help.

Harry Emerson Fosdick wrote in his autobiography that John D. Rockefeller, the man with great wealth, never used his money in a way to hurt the church or to get more leverage or power. He said that in business sessions he had seen Mr. Rockefeller argue against a particular issue, but, once the church had approved it, he would agree to serve as the chairman to carry out the very thing which he had been against originally.

There are many simple ways we can encourage our new pastor and each other. A telephone call can say to a church member: "We have been missing you and hope you can come back soon." Or "I have been thinking about you during this hard time." Or "I am praying for you in your grief." You can say to your new pastor: "I see a bright future for our church." "I'm glad you are here, and I look forward to working with you." "Thank you for that sermon. It helped me or comforted me." Drop him a note; send an email; call him and express your encouragement and support. There are so many ways we can say we care or appreciate him and each other.

Carlyle Marney spoke about a young girl who was going to a progressive school and had gotten a B or C in chemistry, which is a difficult subject. She had a hard time in the course, and the teacher put this note on her report card: "We can't all be chemists, but we would all like to be Susans." She might not be great in chemistry, but she was somebody that the teacher could affirm as a person. We need to affirm each other in the variety of gifts which we have. Let's seek to find that role of affirmation for your new pastor and his family.

AFFIRM YOUR PASTOR'S SINCERE MINISTRY ROLE

5) A phrase which is thrown around rather loosely, when describing another person's motives, is the one which depicts him or her as being either sincere or insincere. Insincerity is a rather harsh criticism while sincerity is a lofty demand. Consider the origin of

the word *sincere*. In the Greco-Roman world marble pillars were often found with flaws in some of them. Unscrupulous sellers filled the cavities with wax and polished over them, so the wax blended in with the rest of the marble, and they were sold as sound. When the impact of the natural elements beat upon them, the wax eroded away, and the flaws were revealed. These pillars were not *sine cera*. They were not without wax. When we sign a letter, and say I am sincerely yours," we are declaring that we are "without wax." We are what we claim to be. To be sincere is to be real, genuine, unvarnished, pure, unalloyed, or unmixed. The pure in heart are sincere; they are without wax.

It is, of course, easy to sign a letter "Sincerely yours," but it is much more difficult to let our words on paper or in sound harmonize with our life. True sincerity is not merely an exercise to persuade someone else that we are honest and noble. Genuine sincerity arises out of a life filled with conviction and integrity. It is a living thing that emerges out of who we are within. Sincerity, if real, pervades a person's whole being and is the foundation of one's character. To be sincere is to reveal a sound character. Insincerity exposes a disfigurement within which no external pretense can long disguise. Affirm your pastor's sincere ministry and offer your own sincerity as well.

BE TOLERANT OF ONE ANOTHER

6) *Be tolerant of each other.* Paul says we also are to be tolerant. We learn to speak the truth in love. That does not mean that we never criticize or desire to see things differently. But we should express our feelings in love. Any word of criticism does not seek to hurt or harm someone else. The one person I am really frightened of, and am convinced does not really understand the Christian faith, is the one who says that he or she is the only one who has the whole truth or the whole gospel. All of us are in the process of growing, understanding, and developing in maturity.

Tolerance permits us to be open to a brother or sister who may have a new insight for us. Our life might be enriched by those with whom we differ, if we learn to disagree in grace and love. Although we see things differently and interpret them differently, we do not deny that they are not a part of the Body of Christ. I pray that you will continue to be open and growing, listening and learning.

UNITY IN DIVERSITY

7) Paul reminds us that there is *unity in diversity.* There are many parts of the human body. The body is not made up of the ear or the eye or the feet or the legs alone. They all are a part of the whole body. In the Body of Christ, each has a part in the unity of the whole. Your part—your ministry—is important in the life of this church. It is vital! Do not say or do anything that hurts the unity of the church or would cause divisiveness within the congregation. Be a healer, comforter and one who unites not divides.

THE IMPORTANCE OF PRAYER

8) *We can also pray.* We say so often that we ought to pray. I believe in the power of prayer, and I do not believe that things are the same without prayer. I think that when you and I pray we open ourselves to the power of God which is available to come into our lives. As we open our lives to God, God can work through us more creatively than if we do not pray.

I hope you will pray, and that you will pray for your new pastor and his family, and I know that he will pray for you. Those of you who cannot come to church because of health, you can also pray. That can be one of your ways of sharing in the ongoing ministries of this church right now. There is nothing more encouraging for us than for someone to say, "I am praying for you."

GOD'S CHURCH IN THE WORLD

Why do we do ministry? Paul says that we do all of our work to be of service for Christ. We are seeking to *equip ourselves, so we might be God's Church in the world.* We are engaged in ministry as partners in service. We labor not for ourselves but for what we can do for Christ. Our deeds are our words. Our words are transformed into action so that others can see that we are living out the life of Christ in the world. We are to bring Christ to touch the world where we live.

We seek to follow the Christ who has called us into a ministry of service. Like our Lord who took up the towel and basin, we follow Him in service. If we do not follow Him in service, then we will leave the woman at the well. We will leave the beggar at the gate. We will leave the blind man in his darkness. We will leave the deaf man in a soundless world. We will leave Mary and Martha in their grief. We will leave the Matthews of life at the tax collector's desk. We are called to pick up the towel and basin and go into the world to serve in the name of Jesus Christ.

In Connecticut there is a state law which requires that all church doors open externally. I like that law. The church gathers in worship to go forth to worship and serve in the world. The most important thing is not just what happens in this building each week. We gather together to learn what it is to be the Church, and then we are to go forth in the world to be the Church in the name of Jesus Christ. We have been called not to receive but to give; to be loving; not to be lavished upon; to be ministering; and not to have others minister unto us. Having felt the power of Christ in our lives, we realize that he has called us to serve in the world.

A VISION OF THE CHURCH

As your new pastor comes in three Sundays, I hope you can capture something anew of *the vision of what the church is.* In these next few weeks, I pray you will catch anew what your ministry, call, and commitment to Christ is. May each person recommit his or her life more fully to Christ.

Many years ago in England, a man stood reading a plaque on a church door. It read: "Here God laid His hands on William

Booth." The man stood there awhile looking at the plaque. Finally, the custodian came over and said: "I'm sorry mister, but it is time to close the church. You need to move on." The man said, "Give me just another moment, please."

The custodian said, "Ok, just another moment." And the man read the plaque again. "Here God laid His hands on William Booth." The custodian suddenly realized that the man reading the plaque was William Booth himself, the founder of the Salvation Army. Then he heard Mr. Booth praying, "O God, do it again. Do it again!"

In some place, quiet or noisy, God laid his hand upon your life, and you committed your life to God. That is not the only time God is supposed to touch your life. We need to pray, "O God, do it again and again." Let my life grow. Let me reach for maturity. Let me seek to become like Christ, who is the Head of the Church that I might grow up to be more like Him. Let us commit our lives to be like Christ and to serve faithfully in His name. May our prayer be: "O God, do it again and again and again."

On this last Sunday of my twenty months of ministry with you, I thank you for your support and urge you to give thanks for your new pastor, Dr. Charles Jones, that you have called to serve in ministry with you and to offer your prayer of thanksgiving for him and your opportunity to minister together. May God bless Charles and Donna Jones and you as a church.

O Father God, we thank you for your love which goes beyond our imagination, and your grace that stretches us beyond what we deserve. May we now take up our crosses as we follow the Christ, who died for us, that we might live the sacrificial life in the world as we serve and love in His name. Amen.

PASTORAL PRAYER

O God of all places and especially known in this place by so many through the years, we lift our spirits to commune with Your Divine Spirit today. Give us a strong sensitivity to Your Presence. We long to be assured that You are with us today. Speak to our mind, stir our emotions, inspire our enthusiasm, encourage our service, direct our actions, motivate our thoughts, strengthen our moral fiber, and touch us with reassurance. We acknowledge our failures and sins and ask for Your forgiveness and strength to withstand the temptations that whirl around us and within us. May the assurance of Your Presence today provide us strength to worship and serve You faithfully.

We thank You for all the pastors and ministers and laypersons who have served You faithfully for almost two centuries in this church. As the church now awaits the coming of its new pastor, Charles Jones, and the new chapter that will enfold with his coming, gird him and these good people with the confidence that You are present with them in this time of transition and new beginnings and will guide them in their ministry in the years ahead. Give them expectancy and hope, confidence and encouragement, enthusiasm and commitment, faith and assurance as this congregation and its new pastor begin their ministry together. May minor differences be put aside as they move forward together in unity of purpose and commitment to serving Christ to the best of one's ability. Bless Charles, Donna, James and Margaret and this congregation with Your love and grace. May they begin a romance of ministry that will grow and blossom over the years. May this be a place where all who come will see the spirit of Christ in the manner, words, thoughts, and behavior of this church family. May the highest desire of all be to serve Christ and not for personal recognition or acclaim.

I thank You for the privilege of serving as Pastor in the Interim in this sacred place. I lift these good people to You in my prayer with confidence that they will continue to serve You faithfully here. I have sensed their love for Christ and His Church and for their desire to serve. Fortify that intent with Your Constant Presence and guidance. Comfort us always with the assurance that nothing ever separates us from Your Presence. Through Christ who goes before us, we pray. Amen.

ACTION AND REFLECTION

Encourage your group to share with one another the way certain lay persons have helped strengthen their local church or have influenced them individually in a positive way for ministry or have been harmful in the church's ministry.

DISCUSSION

1. What does it mean to speak of every Christian as a priest?

2. Define how you see the role of laity in your church?

3. Name some positive ways you believe lay persons can assist the pastor in ministry?

4. How do you envision the church engaging in your local community and in the larger world for Christ?

5. How do you confront the negativity which many persons seem to have toward the church today?

CHAPTER 3

THE STORY GOES ON

GENESIS 1: 27; MARK 16:1-7

I am sure that you, like I, have been reading a magazine or watching a television program when it was flashed on the screen, or you came to the last page and the article or TV said, "Continued." In a way life is a continued story. It is never full and complete just in one moment. Life is learning to go on with the story. We draw on what we already know about the story and then keep on telling the story. "Life is lived best," Elton Trueblood said, "when it is lived in chapters." I am concluding a chapter in my life with you, and this church is concluding a chapter in its history with me. We have shared almost seven years together. Sometimes in these continued stories there is a brief synopsis given of what has gone on before the new segment is picked up. I want to take a few moments this morning and give a few clippings from the past before the story is continued.

THE GOSPEL STORY

The gospel story is carried on by people. It is not just my story or your story. It is *the* story. We tell our stories as we try to point people to *the* story about what God has done in Christ. You, as members of this congregation, have been a part of my story for almost seven years. I have discovered that this church is filled with many dedicated people who are willing to serve in many places—some without acknowledgement or thanks. Some of you have labored for many years as teachers in Sunday School classes, choir and mission leaders, and have stood by this church through many years in good times and in bad times, have served on committees or other places, with little recognition and you have done it all for the glory of God. Thank you for your commitment and service in and through First Baptist Church.

I want to say to all of you who have supported my ministry and encouraged us during our years with you a special word of thanks and appreciation. As we say goodbye, I want to say thanks to those who encouraged Emily and me and stood by us and brightened us with your laughter and joy, prayed for us, loved us and supported our ministry. We appreciated you and will remember you with fondness through the years. My wife, Emily, has worked beside me, shared her gifts faithfully here and been my chief source of strength. Her love, encouragement, and support have sustained me. She is a special person and I know I have been blessed to have her as my wife.

In a way the gospel is always given to us in installments. We receive installments from those who went before us, and then we in turn pass the gospel on to others. I have done that with you. As I reflect back over these seven years with you, let me remind you of some of those things that I have attempted to share with you and the other churches I have served during these forty-five years of ministry. I hope you will pass these comments on to others who will follow.

THE LIBERATING NATURE OF THE GOSPEL

First, I have tried to share with you the liberating nature of the Gospel of Jesus Christ. God's message comes to us as Good

News. God's love and grace free us from our sins. If you had cancer and were in the hospital and someone came into the room and told you that they had found a cure for cancer, that would be liberating news.

David H.C. Read spent five years as a prisoner of war in the German concentration camp. In 1945 the news began to spread through the prison camp, "The Americans are coming! The Americans are coming!" Soon the Americans were there. The prisoners saw the American army coming in the distance. First, they saw the soldiers and then the tanks of General Patton. They knew that liberation had come. The Christian gospel is the good news of liberation. It is liberation from sin, guilt, and anxiety. It is good news that God loves you and God loves me. We are to accept our acceptance by God. This is one of the great affirmations of the Christian faith. You and I are loved and can be liberated. That is *the* Good News.

THE JOY OF THE GOOD NEWS

Second, I have tried to emphasize the joy of this Good News. For too long, many persons have suffered under negative preaching. We have been whipped to death with our sins, and preachers have played upon our guilt and emotions. The faces of many persons have been rubbed in their sins. Many of us have left worship services like whipped dogs with our tail between our legs. With this negative, hell-fire, damnation preaching, the preacher may have felt better, but everybody else felt worse. The gospel of Jesus Christ is not meant to make us feel bad. It is good news of great joy. Christ has come that we might have life and have it more abundantly.

The kind of joy that Jesus Christ gives us is an internal joy. It is not joy made up of clichés and superficiality. It is the kind of joy that sustains us in difficult, hard times. It is that inner joy which comes from the presence of God that sustains us in the face of rejection, obstacles, difficulties, suffering, pain, or even death. It is the joy that comes from the assurance that nothing ultimately separates us from the love of God when we are in Jesus Christ our Lord.

When we search the Scriptures, we do not find evidence that our Lord Jesus Christ ever attempted to put people down because of their sins. To the woman at the well, he offered forgiveness. To Zacchaeus up a tree, he offered forgiveness. To the woman caught in the act of adultery, Jesus said, "Neither do I condemn you. Go and sin no more." The harshest words of condemnation which Jesus directed were always at those who thought they were OK. These people took pride in their religion, but they were hypocrites. They thought they had no more need of God. Jesus spoke to them harshly. But to some of the worst so called sinners in society, Jesus expressed love, forgiveness, and hope. All of us need to be reminded that the gospel is good news of great joy. Let us not be as C. S. Lewis was, "surprised by the joy of the faith." Let us affirm it, accept it, and rejoice in the wonderful grace of God.

IMPORTANCE OF WORSHIP

Third, another central emphasis has been on worship. Worship is the most important act the church does. Worship is our way of offering praise and adoration to God and responding to God's presence. I have attempted to lead us into a deeper understanding of what biblical worship is. I have reminded you that worship is not something God does for us but what we do for God. Worship is not so much seeing what we can get God to do for us but what we do for God. We praise God, adore God, love God, and serve God. We do not worship so the preacher or other persons can be glorified, affirmed or applauded, but in order to affirm God and discover what God wants us to do. That is the reason I have always felt that the preacher and other staff members should never be at the center of worship. We do not call attention to ourselves, but we seek to glorify God in everything we do in this place.

This sanctuary has been designed to point people to God. Our attempt at worship calls us to sense the wonder of God. Our God is a holy God. We kneel before God in holiness, aware that we are sinners saved by grace. We worship a God who is a big God, and who lovingly responds to us, not because we are worthy, but because God is a God of love. Our God bridges the chasm that separates us because of our sins and seeks to draw us in love to God's self.

Let me challenge you to continue working on your inner-life—your spiritual core. Remember the importance of prayer and personal devotions. The quiet time spent with God is essential for spiritual development. We never outgrow the need for private or corporate spiritual nourishment. Make the time for your prayer life, be faithful to it and do not forsake the importance of weekly worship with fellow believers in Church. It is too easy to let everything else push these important times from our lives.

Worship is an oasis in time. We set apart a segment of time to focus our lives on the eternal God of the universe. We worship to draw on the strength and power of God's presence to face the difficulties of life, as well as to express our thanksgiving. The word, "sabbath" comes from an old Babylonian word which means "stop doing what you normally do." Every one of us needs to stop doing what he or she normally does in one's work or play and focus upon God so that each of us can draw the power of God's presence into our lives. We need worship as surely as our eyes need light to see, our ears need sound to hear, our lungs need air to breathe, and the body needs food to sustain it.

THE PRIESTHOOD OF THE BELIEVERS

Fourth, I have also affirmed the priesthood of Believers. When this belief is put into practice, the church will know that ministry is not just for professional holy persons but the responsibility of *all* persons. The primary role of the pastor is to be an equipper. He is one who trains and guides all Christians into their own ministry. I am not the only minister in this church. The professional staff are not the only ministers in this church. We have hundreds of ministers in this congregation. Every single member is a minister for Jesus Christ. The real ministry of the church will be lay-led.

Remember that Jesus Himself was a layperson. He called around him twelve persons who were all lay ministers. Stephen and Barnabas were lay ministers. Although Paul was a rabbi, he always made his own living by making tents. Most of the work of the church is done by laypersons. YOU, not professionals, are the real ministers.

In this church, I see faithful men and women who go to our nursing homes and touch the lives of the many people there. I see Sunday School workers, who have taught preschoolers for years. I see the friendly hand of deacons and others extended to me and others as we come in the door on Sunday morning. I see greeters standing at the front door welcoming people as they come to worship. I see many faces who have always been encouragers. I see those involved in our "Inasmuch" and other local ministries and hundreds of other laypersons in this church who serve faithfully in the name of Christ. The real ministry of Christ cannot be limited to the work of a few professionals. Christ has called all of us into ministry. Affirm your gifts and find your place of service.

CREATED IN THE IMAGE OF GOD TO GROW SPIRITUALLY

Fifth, remember that you have been created in the image of God (Genesis 1: 27) and challenged to continue your spiritual growth. You and I are called to the highest standards—to be like God. To love God with all of one's heart, mind, strength, and soul is the call to excellence. It is a reminder of our creation. To remember who you are is to recognize that you are a child of God, created in God's image.

But we have not arrived. We are reaching toward becoming what God has created us to be, as full authentic persons, real human beings. How often we say, "Aw, I was only human," as though that is not to be anything very worthy. To talk about becoming human is to realize what God has created you to be as God's child. It is the challenge to be a full, complete, whole person as we were created to be. Keep on growing as you love God with all of your being. Our experience of new birth in Christ was the beginning. It was not the end. We are to keep on growing and developing.

To love God with all our being is to be aware that our spiritual development is never complete. Each of us is always in the process of becoming. The one person I know who is the most spiritually immature is the individual who says that he or she has arrived spiritually. None of us can say, "I'm done with my spiritual development." No one ever *really* is! In the process of becoming, we either go forward or backward. There is no area of neutrality. We are either growing and moving forward so that our mind, heart, and being are progressing or we are regressing, moving backwards. Jesus has challenged us to be perfect—to reach for the highest we can be. We are always growing spiritually.

To love God with all your being is to hold before yourself the awareness of what you can become. It is to learn to live with God at your elbow. It is to live with the power of God's presence breaking into your life. It is to realize that the challenge of learning is ever before you and beyond you. Robert Hofstadter, a Nobel Prize winner in physics, expressed it well a decade or so ago: "Many will never find the end of the trail. It is ever before you and pulling you toward the not yet realized."

I have challenged you "to love God with all your mind" as well as "with all your heart." It is easy to allow our emotions to reign in our spiritual growth. We indeed need to "feel" deeply about our belief. We need to have "tender hearts" but we also need "tough minds," as William James has reminded us. I believe that God wants us to use our brains in God's service. Hegel has reminded us that "to think and to think hard is a religious duty."

A devout "Believer" does not have to be divorced from a good "thinker." Down through history there have always been dedicated Christians who have given their minds as well as their hearts in service to God and truth. Christians like Paul, Athanasius, Augustine, Aquinas, Luther, Barth, Schweitzer, Rauschenbusch, Baillie, Tillich, and thousands of others have believed that to love God with all one's mind is not separate from what it means to be Christian. A growing Christian does not believe anything or everything or respond to every sentimental or emotional appeal. He or she is committed to loving God with all of one's mind and acknowledges that as a sacred duty.

LOVE AND CARE FOR ONE ANOTHER

Sixth, another emphasis that I have tried to encourage you to undertake is the need to love and care for others in the name of Christ. Many of you have done that so graciously in the time of need in the life of other people. Numerous persons have told me how much their Sunday School class or individuals have meant to them in a time of some crisis. You brought food, comforted them in the hospital, you sat with their children, you stayed up all night with them, you gave them transportation. You served in so many ways.

A man was asked once, "Which is the worst problem in the world? Apathy or ignorance?" The man thought for a moment and then said, "I don't know and I don't care." Unfortunately, apathy and ignorance are two of the worst problems that exist. I suppose one of the worst attitudes of all could be "I couldn't care less." I believe that it is a sin simply not to care enough about others. In the name of Christ, we are called to minister and help. It is not enough to talk about love. Love has to be seen in action. As James says, "Faith without works is dead." I have seen many of you express this kind of love to others by your actions in times of need. You have embraced persons when they were hurting, lifted them when they were down, comforted them when grieving, cheered them when they were blue, and guided them when they needed direction. Love has been multiplied through your concern.

Remember that the important ministries of the church need to be done in the community where the church reaches beyond the boundaries of its walls and seeks to make a difference in the city where it is. What happens inside these walls in worship and training is to equip us to take the good news into the world and change the lives of people who are there. We also go into the world working with other religious groups, seeking to combine our efforts with theirs to combat the forces of evil.

As you labor, seek to be inclusive and not exclusive. We will be stronger as we work with fellow believers no matter what their religious tradition is. We do not assume that we have all the truth about God but link our hands with all those who love God to seek to overcome evil with good, to correct injustices, to right wrongs, to overcome bigotry and prejudice, and to meet human needs.

A CALL TO SERVICE

If you and I are to do the work and ministry of Christ, we have to recognize that it is a call to service. I suppose one of the saddest things in any kind of organization would be for people to work primarily for whatever glory or recognition they received from it. The call from Jesus Christ is a summons to be a servant. Jesus said that "the greatest of all is the servant of all." One of the finest programs we have in our church is our deacon flock ministry. In this program, the deacons are called to be servants, to reach out and minister in the name of Christ to see what they can do to help others. I hope this ministry will continue. We serve not so much to have light shine on us, but so that we can cast light on Christ. Our lives should reflect Christ and not simply call attention to ourselves.

There is a story that comes out of Tibet. A group went to Tibet on a mission. Their guide or servant was a man named Leo. Leo was responsible for doing the menial tasks—the cooking, carrying of the baggage, and setting up the tents. The people on this mission trip were always warmed and refreshed by his enthusiasm, his songs in the night, his willingness to do the most menial tasks and his positive attitude. At one point the group experienced a shipwreck, and they were separated from part of the group. They suddenly realized that Leo was no longer present. They tried to continue their journey, but they were not able to go on without the work and support of Leo. They came back to see the tribal chief and to tell him that they were no longer able to continue the journey. When they met the chief, they were astounded to see that the tribal chief was Leo. The one that they thought was their servant had been their king.

This is a parable. Those who are really the most kingly in nature are those who are willing to serve. They realize that there is no such thing as an insignificant place to serve. As we work for Christ wherever we are, we labor to serve and honor Christ and we honor ourselves by following his love and grace. We serve the One who was willing to serve, even to the point of laying down his life for the Church.

If we are to serve Christ faithfully, our ministry cannot be limited to our work in Sunday School, church committees, and other places in the local church, as important as these are. We are challenged to serve Christ through our vocations, business, recreation, family life and in all areas of our life. People must see in our daily life that what we say and do on Sunday affects our business life and all the rest of our living in the Christian principles of personal respect, honesty, integrity, and high moral values that are evident in our lives. This calls for what Reinhold Niebuhr, the theologian, described as being "moral men (persons) in an immoral society." This calls for persons whose word is their bond, their handshake on a deal a promise guaranteed, their integrity without question, their character above reproach, and their ethical behavior a model for the highest values. We cannot separate our religious life from our daily work and relationships with others. William Carey, who became the first Baptist missionary, said: "I cobble shoes to make a living, but my primary purpose is to serve Christ." Whatever way you make a living, remember your central purpose is to witness and serve Christ through that labor.

As we strive to serve Christ, remember Christ is our model, our standard, our guide, and our example. After Jesus finished washing his disciples' feet at the Last Supper, he told them: "For I have set you an example that you also should do as I have done to you" (John 13:15). Jesus went as far as to lay down his life for us. To follow the example of Jesus, we seek to serve without looking for reward, recognition, commendation, praise, gratitude, or something in return. In following Christ—You and I serve because there is a need,

> a job to be done,
>> a burden to be borne,
>>> a grief to be shared,
>>>> a heart to be uplifted,
>>>>> a depressed spirit to be cheered,
>>>>>> a weak faith to be renewed,

You and I serve to follow our Master Teacher, and Lord, Jesus Christ.

In one of my congregations there was an older woman, who was without family and was home-bound and asked church members for assistance frequently. After driving this woman to the doctor one day, bringing her some groceries, and furnishing her a meal, the church member, who had helped this elderly woman, was met by another church member later. "Why do you do anything for Mrs. Blank," she asked. "She doesn't appreciate anything you do for her." The helpful woman replied quietly, "I don't do it to be appreciated. I do it because there is a need." This woman understood the role of a servant—one does not serve to be thanked, affirmed, or appreciated, but because there is a genuine need. We are called to be servants!

THE CHURCH AS A FELLOWSHIP

Seventh, the Church is also a community. It is a fellowship. It is a group of people who reach out to one another to draw strength from each other. As Paul reminds us, "We are bonded and knit together, no longer aliens, strangers, but we are fellow citizens."

We belong now to the community. We are not strangers; we are a part of the family. That is what the church is—family, working together as followers of our Lord.

One of my favorite stories is the one where Charlie Brown and Lucy are sitting in front of the television set. Lucy comes in and changes channels and Charlie Brown looks up at her and says, "I was watching that program. What gives you the right to come in here and change the station?" Lucy lifts up her hand and says, "See this hand. Individually these fingers are not much. But when brought together like this, they become a force mighty to behold." Then Charlie Brown says, "That's reason enough."

In the church individually, you and I are always weak. Whenever the church is divided it is weakened. It needs to be united in love and grace. As a community of faith, we provide strength to others in times of difficulty and need and affirm one another in times of happiness and progress.

PERSONAL REFLECTIONS

Thank you also for supporting my personal participation in community affairs outside the church like Rotary, the Boys and Girls Club, the Family Counseling Center, the Chamber of Commerce board, the trustee boards of a college and seminary, and involvement in ecumenical ministries, interfaith councils, as well as our local and state Baptist committees and associations, committees on the Baptist World Alliance, the Baptist AIDS Partnership, among others. I hope you will encourage your new pastor to engage in such ministries outside the church.

Emily and I are now going to begin an exciting new chapter in our lives—the chapter of retirement. We do not know what we shall do yet nor where we will live, likely somewhere near Richmond, Virginia. We hope to spend more time with our children and grandchildren and await whatever doors the Lord will open to us. We step into the future in good health and in good spirits with a strong sense of calling and excitement about this new venture. In the past years, I have believed strongly in the providence of God, and that same assurance will carry us across the bridge into the next phase of our life.

THE FUTURE IS A FRIEND

I want to leave you with this final word—the future is a friend. You need not fear it. This church still has wonderful opportunities in front of it. You are a marvelous people, with many gifts. You can do great things for this church as you commit yourself to God. Right now, the future is unknown, but you will place your hand in the hand of God assured that God will be there to go with you.

Do you remember when the women arrived at the tomb to anoint the body of Jesus, that they were concerned about the stone that was blocking the grave? "How can we remove that stone?" they had asked on the way. But when they arrived at the tomb, they discovered that the stone was already removed. They did not have to deal with a dead body. They discovered that Christ was risen. The angel said to them that he had gone before them. "He is not here. He is risen and gone before you." As you move into the future, move into it with the assurance that God is present with you, and that he goes before you to guide you into whatever lies before you.

One day a little boy whose right arm had been amputated at the elbow came to visit in a children's Sunday School class. The teacher of the class wanted to be sensitive to his situation and tried to choose activities in which the boy could participate.

Toward the end of the class session, the teacher asked the girls and boys to form a circle and sing some songs and choruses. She finally announced, "Let's do the church song: Here is the church, here is the steeple, open the doors and see all the people." As the children prepared to do the actions which accompany the words, the teacher became uneasy because she realized that, for the moment, she had forgotten the new boy whose arm had been amputated.

As she wondered how to lessen the hurt which he certainly would experience, a little girl sitting beside him took charge of the situation. She said to the boy, "Here, with my hand and yours we shall make the church."

The church that God would build here, God will build with the hands of all of you. Join your hands together, place your hands in God's hand and you will have the assurance of God's grace and guidance into the future. May God bless you to do it.

God bless these people to be your church in this place in this time. Thank you for these years of ministry we have shared together. Guide them as they go on with the story.

PASTORAL PRAYER

Gracious God, we pause now to thank You for the years that we have shared together as pastor and people. We acknowledge our joys and sorrows, our victories and defeats, our accomplishments and struggles, our faith and doubts. Thank You for the lessons learned and jobs accomplished. We thank You for willing workers and loyal members; for people who have stood by and will continue to stand by the church they love. We thank you for those who have given of their time, talents, and devotion.

We pause now to remember those this morning who are no longer with us because of death. We remember their love and devotion to this church and the vacancies which they leave. We thank You for the lengthening shadows for good which they have left across the path of this church and our lives. We acknowledge our loss but affirm our faith in the abundant life eternal.

Bless those this day who are hurting, who are lonely, depressed, sad, weak, weary, and alone. Bless those who face surgery. May they have a strong sense of Your sustaining presence. Sustain those who grieve.

We thank You for the joy and wonder of the faith we have in Christ. We thank You for the abundant life and the assurance of Your daily presence. Thank You for loving us even when we are unlovable. Thank You for accepting us even when we are unacceptable. Thank You for giving us the courage to keep on keeping on when the way is hard. Let the radiance of the joy of Your presence shine through the windows of our spirits this day. May Your presence warm our lives in such a way that we will live for You and serve You more lovingly.

Bless now this church. Thank You for allowing me to serve as their pastor. Bless the good people of this congregation with Your love and grace. Guide them as they seek a new pastor. Direct the interim committee and the pastor search committee. May they sense the power of Your leadership in all that they do. Through Christ our Lord, we pray. Amen.

ACTION AND REFLECTION

Assume that your pastor has just completed fifteen years of successful ministry in your church before he or she retires or accepts a calling to another church. To what do you attribute his or her success--preaching, pastoral care, or what? What role in a positive or negative way did the laity have in the success of that ministry?

DISCUSSION

1. What do you see as the essential nature of the Gospel that is proclaimed from the pulpit?

2. Should worship take a prominent role in the pastor's preparation? In what particular ways should he or she prepare for worship, and what should be the role for laity in the preparation for worship?

3. How do you interpret the concept of the "fellowship" of the church? How significant is the role of laity in the fellowship of the church?

4. How do you think your church will face the future now that your pastor has retired or moved to another church? What will

be some of the necessary steps that will need to be undertaken to address this issue?

5.   How do you interpret the meaning of the concept of serving in Jesus' name?

EPILOGUE

The coming of a new pastor is usually an exciting and challenging opportunity in the life of a congregation. The interim or transitional period before the new pastor arrives is a time usually filled with anticipation, worry, frustration, fear, uncertainty, hope, and many other feelings. Used appropriately by the interim pastor and church committees and the church at large, this time can be of immense importance to the congregation. Following the leaving of the last pastor, the church often confronts various attitudes, some positive and others negative. Some experience grief at the departure of the last pastor, while others may be happy for the change. If a congregation wishes to remain healthy and vital, this occasion can afford the church a chance to make solid preparations before the new pastor comes. It would be wise for the church to examine their history and determine what their roots have been and whether they are travelling on a similar path today as a congregation.

This time is also useful for the congregation to examine their identity. Are they really who they think they are in their worship style, in their denominational linkage, community and neighborhood image, and age assessment? Are they dominated by the former pastor's personality and theological perspective; or are they a caring and supportive congregation of one another, or are they reserved and uninvolved? Would their assessment of themselves be the major factor in what they look for in a new pastor or would they be open to change and someone different? Are they set in their ways and resistant to change of any kind, especially in their type of pastor?

The interim time is also a juncture to examine the church's leadership style and ascertain who their main leaders are. Is the church riddled with conflict and division or is it resolved to work together in a healthy way as they look for a new pastor? With proper leadership, the church can resolve to bring closure to the former pastor's tenure and plan to move united in a new direction to find a pastor who will be a good match for the congregation as they genuinely understand who they are.

The beginning and ending of a pastorate are critical occasions in the ongoing life of a congregation. The sermons I have offered as examples in this book are provided to suggest ways one might assist a church during this transition. They are a resource for congregational leaders and pastors dealing with a pastor's departure or the beginning of a new pastorate. As I indicated earlier, however, the exiting pastor or interim pastor must also work with committees and the church at large in a personal way to help them plan how they will meet this transition as they prepare for the new chapter with their next pastor. I believe careful preparation for these transitions can make the next chapter in the church a more positive one. As we labor in building the church, remember the words of the Apostle Paul: "According to the grace of God given to me, like a skilled master builder I laid a foundation, and someone else is building on it. Each builder must choose with care how to build on it. For no one can lay any foundation other than the one that has been laid, that foundation is Jesus Christ" (1 Corinthians 3: 10-11).

A Charge To The Pastoral Candidate

I charge you to deepen your relationship with Christ through your personal devotion and prayers each day.

I charge you to search the Scriptures that you might grow in your knowledge of Christ and his way.

I charge you to continue to grow in your knowledge of ministry by continuous study and special educational opportunities.

I charge you to commit your life humbly to serve Christ, who said that the greatest of all is the servant of all.

I charge you to guide your church to follow the Christ-like way.

I charge you to love the Church, warts, and all.

I charge you to love the people with whom you minister.

I charge you to guard time for your family.

I charge you to care for your health through regular exercise.

I charge you to be open to God's spirit and the surprising ways God might lead you and your congregation.

I charge you to love God with all your heart, soul, mind, and strength, and your neighbor as yourself.

A CHARGE TO THE CONGREGATION

I charge you to strive to follow the Christ-like way in all your ministry.

I charge you to be faithful in worship and in your biblical studies to grow in the knowledge of Christ and his teachings.

I charge you to use your spiritual gifts in ministry through your church and in your community.

I charge you to respect and support your fellow members in good and difficult times.

I charge you to love and support your pastor, and work together to discern the guidance of Christ for your particular ministries in your congregation and in your community and beyond.

I charge you to allow your pastor the time and space for personal spiritual meditation and growth.

I charge you to grant your pastor needed leisure time and grant him appropriate time with his family.

I charge you to give your pastor a free pulpit and the required responsibility to share the Gospel as it relates to the needs of the congregation and the challenges of society today.

I charge you to minister with your pastor in the pastoral care of your congregation.

I charge you to love God with all your heart, soul, mind, and strength, and your neighbor as yourself.

BIBLIOGRAPHY

Bagby, Daniel G. *Crisis Ministry: A Handbook*. Macon GA: Smyth & Helwys, 2002.

Bass, Diana Butler. *Christianity for the Rest of Us: How the Neighborhood Church Is Transforming the Faith*. San Francisco: HarperSanFrancisco, 2006.

Bendroth, Norman B., editor. *Transitional Ministry: Successful Strategies for Churches and Pastors*. Herndon VA: The Alban Institute, 2014.

Bennett, J. Sims. *Servanthood: Leadership for the Third Millennium*. Cambridge MA: Cowley Publications, 1997.

Bratcher, Edward B. *The Walk on Water Syndrome: Dealing with Professional Hazards in the Ministry*. Waco TX: Word Books, 1982.

Calian, Carnegie Samuel. *The Spirit-Driven Leader: Seven Keys to Succeeding Under Pressure*. Louisville: Westminster John Knox Press, 2010.

Crabtree, J. Russell. *Transition Apperances: Why Much of What We Know About Pastoral Transitions is Wrong* (Westerville, Ohio: Holy Cow! Consulting 2015).

Dale, Robert D. *Leadership for a Changing Church.* Nashville: Abingdon Press, 1998.

———. *Pastoral Leadership.* Nashville: Abingdon Press, 1986.

Engstrom, Ted W., and Edward R. Dayton. *The Christian Executive.* Waco TX: Word Books, 1979.

Epperly, Bruce G. *Starting with Spirit: Nurturing Your Call to Pastoral Leadership.* Lanham: Rowman & Littlefield, 2010.

Farris, Patricia. *Five Faces of Ministry: Pastor, Parson, Healer, Prophet, Pilgrim.* Nashville: Abingdon, 2015.

Forman, Rowland, Jeff Jones, and Bruce Miller. *The Leadership Baton.* Grand Rapids MI: Zondervan 2004.

Galindo, Israel. *Perspectives on Congregational Leadership.* Vienna VA: Educational Consultants, 2009.

———. *The Hidden Lives of Congregations.* Herndon VA: The Alban Institute, 2004.

Groff, Kent Ira. *Clergy Table Talk.* Gonzalez FL: Energion Publications, 2012.

Heifetz, Ronald. *Leadership without Easy Answers.* Cambridge, MA: Harvard University Press, 1998.

———. Marty Linsky and Alexander Grashow. *The Practice of Adaptive Leadership: Tools and Tactics for Changing Your Organization and the World.* Cambridge MA: Harvard Business Press, 2009).

Hoge, Dean R., and Jacqueline E. Wenger. *Pastors in Transition: Why Clergy Leave Local Church Ministry.* Grand Rapids MI: William B. Eerdmans Publishing Company, 2005.

Jinkins, Michael, and Deborah Bradshaw Jenkins. *In Parish Ministry.* New York: The Alban Institute, 1991.

Johnson, Ben Campbell. *Pastoral Spirituality: A Focus on Ministry.* Philadelphia: The Westminster Press, 1988.

Jones, G. Curtis. *The Naked Shepherd.* Waco TX: Word Books, 1979.

Jones, Jeffery D. *Heart, Mind and Strength: Theory and Practice for Congregational Leadership.* Herndon VA: The Alban Institute, 2008.

Killinger, John. *The Tender Shepherd: A Practical Guide for Today's Pastor.* Nashville: Abingdon Press, 1985.

Lutz, Robert R., and Bruce T. Taylor, editors. *Surviving in Ministry.* Mahwah NY: Paulist Press, 1990.

Malcomson, William L., editor. *How to Survive in the Ministry.* Valley Forge: Judson Press, 1982.

Marshall, Myra. *Beyond Termination.* Nashville: Broadman Press, 1990.

McBrien, Richard P. *Ministry: A Theological, Pastoral Handbook.* San Francisco: Harper & Row, 1987.

Mead, Loren B. *Transforming Congregations for the Future.* New York: The Alban Institute, 1994.

Newbigin, Leslie. *The Good Shepherd.* Grand Rapids MI: Eerdmans Publishing Company, 1977.

Nicholson, Roger S., editor. *Temporary Shepherds: A Congregational Handbook for Interim Ministry.* New York: The Alban Institute, 1998.

Oates, Wayne. *The Christian Pastor.* Philadelphia: The Westminster Press, 1982.

Oden, Thomas C. *Becoming a Minister.* New York: Crossroad, 1987.

Osborn, Ronald. *Creative Disarray: Models of Ministry in a Changing America.* St. Louis MO: Chalice Press, 1991.

Oswald, Roy M. *Clergy Self-Care: Finding a Balance for Effective Ministry.* New York: The Alban Institute, 1991.

Powers, Bruce P., editor. *Church Administration Handbook*. Nashville: B & H Publishers, 2008.

Rediger, G. Lloyd. *Clergy Killers: Guidelines for Pastors and Congregations Under Attack*. Inner Grove Heights MN: Logos Productions, 1996.

Schnase, Robert. *Just Say Yes! Unleasing People for Ministry*. Nashville: Abingdon Press, 2015.

Schwartz, Robert M. *Servant Leaders of the People of God*. New York: Paulist Press, 1989.

Seaborn, Joseph, Jr. *A Celebration of Ministry*. Grand Rapids MI: Baker Book House, 1990.

Sherman, Cecil. T*o Be a Good and Faithful Servant: The Life and Work of a Minister*. Macon GA: Smyth & Helwys, 2010.

Sisk, Ronald D. *Surviving Ministry*. Macon GA: Smyth & Helwys, 1997.

Stafford, Gil W. *When Leadership and Spiritual Directions Meet*. New York: Rowman & Littlefield, 2014.

Tuck, William Powell. *A Pastor Preaching: Toward a Theology of the Proclaimed Word*. Macon GA: Nurturing Faith, Inc., 2012.

————. *Overcoming Sermon Block: The Preacher's Workshop*. Gonzalez FL: Energion Publications, 2014.

————. *Star Thrower: A Pastor's Handbook*. Macon, GA: Smyth & Helwys, 2016.

Warlick, Harold C. *How to Be a Minister and a Human Being*. Valley Forge: Judson Press, 1992.

Weese, Caroline and J. Russell Crabtree. *The Elephant in the Room* (San Francisco, CA, Joseey-Bass, 2004)

Willimon, William H. *Clergy and Laity Burnout*. Nashville: Abingdon Press, 1989.

————. *Pastor: The Theology and Practice of Ordained Ministry.*, rev. edition. Nashville: Abingdon Press, 2016.

Woods, C. Jeff. *Congregational MegaTrends*. New York: The Alban Institute, 1996.

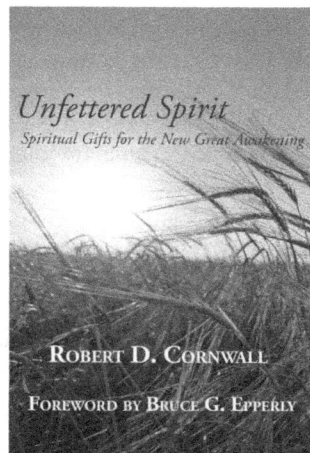

More from Energion Publications

Academy of Parish Clergy Series and Authors

Conversations in Ministry
Clergy Table Talk	Kent Ira Groff	$9.99
Out of the Office	Robert D. Cornwall	$9.99
Wind and Whirlwind	David Moffett-Moore	$9.99

Guides to Practical Ministry
Overcoming Sermon Block	William Powell Tuck	$12.99
Thrive	Ruth Fletcher	$14.99
In Changing Times	Ron Higdon	$14.99
The Space Between	Matthew Braddock	$14.99
Tending the Tree of Life	Richard Voelz	$12.99

Academy Member Authors (Selected Titles)
Faith in the Public Square	Robert D. Cornwall	$16.99
Ultimate Allegiance		$9.99
The Authority of Scripture in a Postmodern Age		$5.99
From Words of Woe to Unbelievable News		$5.99
The Eucharist		$5.99
From Here to Eternity	Bruce Epperly	$5.99
Angels, Mysteries, and Miracles		$9.99
Transforming Acts		$14.99
Jonah: When God Changes		$5.99
Process Theology: Embracing Adventure with God		$5.99
The Journey to the Undiscovered Country	William Powell Tuck	$9.99
Lord, I Keep Getting a Busy Signal		$9.99
The Last Words from the Cross		$9.99
The Church Under the Cross		$9.99
Creation in Contemporary Experience	David Moffett-Moore	$9.99
Life as Pilgrimage		$14.99
The Spirit's Fruit		$9.99
The Jesus Manifesto		$9.99
Spiritual Care Reflections	Charles J. Lopez, Jr.	$14.99
Surviving a Son's Suicide	Ron Higdon	$9.99
All I Need to Know I'm Still Learning at 80		$12.99

Generous Quantity Discounts Available
Dealer Inquiries Welcome
Energion Publications — P.O. Box 841
Gonzalez, FL_ 32560
Website: http://energionpubs.com
Phone: (850) 525-3916